foreword

It's nearly impossible to pick a sun-warmed, garden-ripened tomato without wanting to inhale its wonderful aroma. The scent tells you that you're about to bite into one of summer's essential flavours —how can you resist? No wonder the Italians called them love apples!

True tomato fans know that their favourite fruit—yes, botanically speaking it's a fruit—should never be refrigerated, as it ruins the taste and texture. Keep fresh tomatoes at room temperature, and use them in these delicious recipes from the library of Company's Coming. Your backyard bounty or farmers' market purchases will be the main attraction with these appetizers, soups, salads and entrees. And we've even included some chutneys and jams, so you can savour tomato temptations all year round!

Jean Paré

stuffed cherry tomatoes

These pretty little savouries brighten up any appetizer tray or brunch table.
Use the tip of a teaspoon handle to hollow out the cherry tomatoes.

Salad dressing (or mayonnaise)	2 tbsp.	30 mL
White vinegar	1 tsp.	5 mL
Salt	1/4 tsp.	1 mL
Pepper	1/4 tsp.	1 mL
Dry mustard	1/8 tsp.	0.5 mL
Onion salt	1/8 tsp.	0.5 mL
Finely diced cooked, peeled potato	1 cup	250 mL
Large hard-cooked egg, finely diced	1	1
Green onion, finely chopped	1	1
Finely diced celery	2 tbsp.	30 mL
Cherry tomatoes, halved and seeds removed	34	34

Sprigs of fresh parsley (or dill), for garnish

Combine first 6 ingredients in medium bowl.

Add next 4 ingredients to dressing mixture. Stir to coat.

Spoon about 1 1/2 tsp. (7 mL) potato mixture into each tomato half.

Garnish with parsley. Makes 68 stuffed tomatoes.

1 stuffed tomato: *7 Calories; 0.3 g Total Fat (0.2 g Mono, trace Poly, trace Sat); 3 mg Cholesterol; 1 g Carbohydrate; trace Fibre; trace Protein; 17 mg Sodium*

baked bruschetta

The topping can be made and refrigerated, covered, up to a day ahead. For more Mediterranean flavour, add a minced clove of garlic to the mixture.

Grated mozzarella cheese	1 cup	250 mL
Medium tomatoes, seeds removed and finely diced	2	2
Salad dressing (or mayonnaise)	1/2 cup	125 mL
Chopped pitted whole black olives	1/4 cup	60 mL
Grated Parmesan cheese	1/4 cup	60 mL
Dried oregano	1 tsp.	5 mL
Pepper	1/2 tsp.	2 mL
Dried basil	1/4 tsp.	1 mL
Butter (or hard margarine), softened	1/3 cup	75 mL
Baguette bread slices (1/2 inch, 12 mm, thick)	24	24

Combine first 8 ingredients in medium bowl.

Spread butter on 1 side of each baguette slice. Place, buttered-side up, on baking sheet. Spoon tomato mixture onto baguette slices. Bake in 350°F (175°C) oven for about 15 minutes until hot and cheese is melted. Serve warm. Makes 24 bruschetta.

1 bruschetta: 99 Calories; 7.1 g Total Fat (3.8 g Mono, 1.2 g Poly, 1.7 g Sat); 6 mg Cholesterol; 6 g Carbohydrate; trace Fibre; 2 g Protein; 170 mg Sodium

bruschetta with basil

Perfect for those who can't eat dairy, this appetizer will also have cheese lovers reaching for seconds of this tofu-topped bread. If you can't find a ciabatta loaf, try a baguette, or even a focaccia.

Ciabatta bread loaf, cut into 1/2 inch (12 mm) slices	1	1
Olive oil	1/4 cup	60 mL
Garlic clove, halved	1	1
Medium Roma (plum) tomatoes, seeds removed and chopped	6	6
Finely chopped firm tofu	2/3 cup	150 mL
Finely chopped fresh basil	1/4 cup	60 mL
Olive oil	3 tbsp.	50 mL
Balsamic vinegar	1 tbsp.	15 mL
Garlic clove, minced	1	1
Salt	1/4 tsp.	1 mL
Pepper	1/2 tsp.	2 mL

Lightly brush both sides of bread slices with first amount of olive oil. Place on baking sheet. Broil on top rack in oven for 2 to 3 minutes, turning once, until lightly browned. Rub both sides of bread slices with garlic.

Combine remaining 8 ingredients in medium bowl. Just before serving, spoon tomato mixture onto bread slices. Serves 6.

1 serving: 349 Calories; 20.1 g Total Fat (12.6 g Mono, 3.5 g Poly, 3.0 g Sat); 0 mg Cholesterol; 34 g Carbohydrate; 3 g Fibre; 10 g Protein; 446 mg Sodium

scallop attraction

The combination of scallops, tomatoes and zucchini in this appetizer is downright heavenly!

Hard margarine (not butter)	2 tbsp.	30 mL
Small zucchini (with peel), cut into 1/4 inch (6 mm) slices	2	2
Medium tomatoes, seeds removed and diced	3	3
Dried oregano	1/4 tsp.	1 mL
Dried basil	1/8 tsp.	0.5 mL
Dry (or alcohol-free) white wine	1/4 cup	60 mL
Uncooked large sea scallops, cut in 3 slices each	1 lb.	454 g
Butter (or hard margarine)	2 tbsp.	30 mL
All-purpose flour	2 tbsp.	30 mL
Reserved liquid from scallops	1/3 cup	75 mL
Evaporated skim milk (or half-and-half cream)	2/3 cup	150 mL
Finely diced red pepper or pimiento, for garnish		
Small sprigs fresh basil, for garnish		

Melt margarine in large frying pan on medium. Add zucchini. Cook for about 5 minutes, stirring occasionally, until softened. Transfer to plate.

Add tomato to same frying pan. Cook for about 2 minutes, stirring occasionally, until tomato skin begins to wrinkle. Sprinkle with oregano and basil. Stir. Transfer to separate plate.

Add wine to same frying pan. Bring to a boil. Add scallop slices. Cook for about 2 minutes, stirring occasionally, until scallops are opaque. Transfer scallop slices to plate. Reserve liquid.

Melt butter in small saucepan on medium. Add flour. Heat and stir for 1 minute. Whisk in 1/3 cup (75 mL) reserved liquid from scallops. Slowly add evaporated milk, whisking constantly. Heat and stir until boiling and thickened. Keep warm. To assemble, overlap zucchini slices in circles on 4 plates. Spoon tomato over top. Overlap scallop slices on tomato. Lay 1 scallop slice on top. Pour milk mixture over top.

Garnish with red pepper and basil sprig. Serves 4.

1 serving: 281 Calories; 12.6 g Total Fat (4.8 g Mono, 1.9 g Poly, 4.7 g Sat); 54 mg Cholesterol; 16 g Carbohydrate; 2 g Fibre; 24 g Protein; 352 mg Sodium

mushroom garlic pizza

The Roasted Tomato Sauce is also dynamite with polenta slices or even as a dip. If you don't have a pizza pan, you can always use a baking sheet.

Unbaked pizza crust (12 inch, 30 cm diameter)		
ROASTED TOMATO SAUCE		
Roma (plum) tomatoes, halved lengthwise	6	6
Granulated sugar	2 tsp.	10 mL
Dried crushed chilies	1/2 tsp.	2 mL
Salt	1/2 tsp.	2 mL
Pepper	1/4 tsp.	1 mL
Olive (or cooking) oil	1 tbsp.	15 mL
Finely chopped onion	1/2 cup	125 mL
Garlic cloves, minced (or 1/2 tsp., 2 mL, powder)	2	2
Butter (or hard margarine)	1 1/2 tbsp.	25 mL
Olive (or cooking) oil	2 tsp.	10 mL
Sliced fresh mixed mushrooms (such as white, brown, shiitake, oyster)	3 cups	750 mL
Garlic cloves, minced (or 1/2 tsp., 2 mL, powder)	2	2
Crumbled feta cheese (about 2 1/2 oz., 70 g)	1/2 cup	125 mL
Grated Parmesan cheese	1/2 cup	125 mL
Chopped fresh basil	2 tbsp.	30 mL

Place crust on greased 12 inch (30 cm) pizza pan.

Roasted Tomato Sauce: Arrange tomato, cut-side up, on wire rack on baking sheet with sides. Combine next 4 ingredients in small cup. Sprinkle over top of tomato halves. Bake in 375°F (190°C) oven for about 45 minutes, until tomato is browned and wilted. Cool slightly.

Heat first amount of olive oil in small frying pan on medium. Add onion and garlic. Cook for about 5 minutes, stirring often, until onion is softened. Cool slightly. Transfer to blender or food processor. Add tomato. Process until smooth. Makes about 1 3/4 cups (425 mL) sauce.

Heat butter and second amount of olive oil in large frying pan on medium-high. Add mushrooms. Cook for 5 to 10 minutes, stirring occasionally, until mushrooms are browned and liquid has evaporated. Add garlic. Heat and stir until fragrant. Remove from heat.

Combine remaining 3 ingredients in small bowl. Spread Roasted Tomato Sauce evenly over crust, almost to edge. Spoon mushroom mixture evenly over sauce. Sprinkle with cheese mixture. Bake on bottom rack in 475°F (240°C) oven for about 15 minutes until bottom of crust is golden brown. Cuts into 8 wedges.

1 wedge: 326 Calories; 13.6 g Total Fat (6.4 g Mono, 1.1 g Poly, 5.1 g Sat); 20 mg Cholesterol; 42 g Carbohydrate; 3 g Fibre; 11 g Protein; 866 mg Sodium

tomato, basil and garlic thin crust pizza

We've included an all-purpose pizza dough recipe here. You can make it a day ahead. Store it, covered, in the fridge. If time's an issue, a store-bought, unbaked pizza shell will save you some steps.

THIN CRUST DOUGH

Warm water	1/4 cup	60 mL
Granulated sugar	1/4 tsp.	1 mL
Active dry yeast	2 tsp.	10 mL
Large egg	1	1
All-purpose flour	1 cup	250 mL
Salt	1/2 tsp.	2 mL
All-purpose flour, approximately	1/4 cup	60 mL

TOPPING

Large Roma (plum) tomatoes, quartered	2	2
Small onion, cut into 6 wedges	1	1
Garlic cloves, unpeeled	4	4
Olive (or cooking) oil	1 tbsp.	15 mL
Granulated sugar	1 tsp.	5 mL
Salt	1/2 tsp.	2 mL
Pepper	1/4 tsp.	1 mL
Balsamic vinegar	2 tsp.	10 mL
Garlic cloves, thinly sliced	2	2
Large Roma (plum) tomatoes, cut into 1/8 inch (3 mm) thick slices	2	2
Chopped fresh basil	1/4 cup	60 mL
Grated Parmesan cheese	2/3 cup	150 mL

Thin Crust Dough: Combine water and sugar in small heavy saucepan. Heat and stir on medium until warm and until sugar is dissolved. Remove from heat. Sprinkle yeast over top. Let stand for 10 minutes.

Stir until yeast is dissolved. Add egg. Whisk to combine.

Combine first amount of flour and salt in large bowl. Make a well in centre. Add yeast mixture to well. Mix, adding second amount of flour, 1 tbsp. (15 mL) at a time if necessary, until dough just comes together. Turn out onto lightly floured surface. Knead for about 5 minutes, adding little or no extra flour, until smooth and elastic. Place dough in large greased bowl, turning once to grease top. Cover with greased waxed paper and tea towel. Let stand in oven with light on and door closed for about 1 hour until dough is doubled in bulk. Turn out onto lightly floured surface. Shape into a ball. Roll out and press in lightly greased 12 inch (30 cm) pizza pan.

Topping: Combine first 7 ingredients in small bowl. Spread in baking sheet with sides. Bake in 350°F (175°C) oven for about 30 minutes, stirring once, until vegetables are softened. Cool slightly. Squeeze flesh from first amount of garlic cloves. Discard skins. Put roasted vegetables into food processor. Add vinegar. Process until smooth. Spread topping evenly over thin crust dough almost to edge.

Scatter remaining 4 ingredients, in order given, over top. Bake on bottom rack in 500°F (260°C) oven for about 15 minutes until bottom of crust is golden brown. Cuts into 8 wedges.

1 wedge: 76 Calories; 2.3 g Total Fat (0.7 g Mono, 0.1 g Poly, 0.8 g Sat); 13 mg Cholesterol; 10.8 g Carbohydrate; 1g Fibre; 3.4 g Protein; 209 mg Sodium

tomato salad

This dressing highlights the sweetness of a fresh summer crop. Present this salad on a platter to make the most of the tomato's wonderful colour.

Medium tomatoes, sliced 1/4 inch (6 mm) thick	4	4
Small red onion, thinly sliced	1	1
Finely shredded basil	3 tbsp.	50 mL
HONEY VINEGAR DRESSING		
Balsamic vinegar	2 tbsp.	30 mL
Olive (or cooking) oil	2 tbsp.	30 mL
Lemon juice	2 tsp.	10 mL
Liquid honey	2 tsp.	10 mL
Garlic clove, minced (or 1/4 tsp., 1 mL, powder)	1	1
Crumbled feta cheese	1/2 cup	125 mL

Arrange tomato and onion slices, slightly overlapping, on platter. Sprinkle with basil.

Honey Vinegar Dressing: Combine first 5 ingredients in jar with tight-fitting lid. Shake well. Makes about 1/3 cup (75 mL) dressing. Drizzle over tomato mixture. Chill, covered, for 1 hour.

Just before serving, sprinkle with cheese. Serves 6.

1 serving: 115 Calories; 8.3 g Total Fat (4.2 g Mono, 0.6 g Poly, 3.1 g Sat); 9 mg Cholesterol; 8 g Carbohydrate; 1 g Fibre; 3 g Protein; 68 mg Sodium

stuffed tomato salad

Here's a lovely lunch served up in a gorgeous, edible bowl. You can substitute tuna for the ham, or leave the protein out altogether and make this a colourful side for supper. Save the tomato pulp for your favourite pasta sauce recipe.

Large tomatoes	6	6
Water	6 cups	1.5 L
Salt	3/4 tsp.	4 mL
Orzo	1 cup	250 mL
Light salad dressing (or light mayonnaise)	1/4 cup	60 mL
Grated red onion	2 tbsp.	30 mL
Prepared mustard	2 tsp.	10 mL
Chopped fresh dill (or 1/4 tsp., 1 mL, dried)	1 tsp.	5 mL
Pepper, sprinkle		
Can of flaked ham, drained	6 1/2 oz.	184 g
Diced celery	1/2 cup	125 mL
Diced green pepper	1/4 cup	60 mL
Jar of pimiento, well drained and chopped	2 oz.	57 mL
Green onions, chopped	2	2

Slice 1/2 inch (12 mm) from top of each tomato. Scoop out pulp and seeds. Invert tomatoes on large plate to drain. Set aside.

Combine water and salt in large saucepan. Bring to a boil. Add orzo. Boil, uncovered, for about 8 to 10 minutes, stirring occasionally, until tender but firm. Drain. Rinse with cold water. Drain. Set aside.

Combine next 5 ingredients in medium bowl.

Add remaining 5 ingredients and orzo. Stir. Spoon into tomato shells. Makes 6 stuffed tomatoes.

1 stuffed tomato: 265 Calories; 6.3 g Total Fat (2.8 g Mono, 1.6 g Poly, 1.1 g Sat); 14 mg Cholesterol; 41 g Carbohydrate; 3 g Fibre; 12 g Protein; 455 mg Sodium

tabbouleh

Tabbouleh (pronounced ta-BOO-lee) comes from the Middle East. True tabbouleh always uses fresh herbs, and bumps the amount of chopped parsley up to a cup (250 mL).

Bulgur, fine grind	1 cup	250 mL
Boiling water	1 cup	250 mL
Medium tomatoes, diced	3	3
Green onions, chopped	3	3
Olive (or cooking) oil	1/4 cup	60 mL
Lemon juice	2 tbsp.	30 mL
Chopped fresh mint	1 tbsp.	15 mL
(or 3/4 tsp., 4 mL, dried)		
Finely chopped fresh parsley	1 1/2 tsp.	7 mL
(or 1/4 tsp., 1 mL, flakes)		
Salt	1 tsp.	5 mL
Pepper	1/4 tsp.	1 mL
Ground allspice	1/8 tsp.	0.5 mL

Measure bulgur into large heatproof bowl. Add boiling water. Let stand, covered, for about 15 minutes until water is absorbed.

Add remaining 9 ingredients. Stir. Serves 4.

1 serving: 277 Calories; 15.2 g Total Fat (10.7 g Mono, 1.5 g Poly, 2.1 g Sat); 0 mg Cholesterol; 33 g Carbohydrate; 5 g Fibre; 5 g Protein; 609 mg Sodium

bean and cashew salad

Fresh tomatoes and green beans create an eye-catching salad for a party on the deck. Increase the amount of chili paste if you'd like a little more heat.

Fresh whole green beans	1/2 lb.	225 g
Halved cherry tomatoes	2 cups	500 mL
Raw cashews, toasted (see Tip, page 64)	1 cup	250 mL
Thinly sliced red onion	3/4 cup	175 mL
LEMON DILL DRESSING		
Olive (or cooking) oil	1/3 cup	75 mL
Lemon juice	3 tbsp.	50 mL
Chopped fresh dill	2 tsp.	10 mL
(or 1/2 tsp., 2 mL, dried)		
Garlic clove, minced	1	1
(or 1/4 tsp., 1 mL, powder)		
Chili paste (sambal oelek)	1/2 tsp.	2 mL
Salt	1/4 tsp.	1 mL

Pour water into large frying pan until about 1 inch (2.5 cm) deep. Bring to a boil. Reduce heat to medium. Add green beans. Boil gently, covered, for about 4 minutes until tender-crisp. Drain. Plunge into ice water until cool. Drain. Transfer to large bowl.

Add next 3 ingredients. Toss.

Lemon Dill Dressing: Combine all 6 ingredients in jar with tight-fitting lid. Shake well. Makes about 1/2 cup (125 mL) dressing. Drizzle over bean mixture. Toss well. Serves 8.

1 serving: 211 Calories; 18 g Total Fat (11.9 g Mono, 2.3 g Poly, 3 g Sat); 0 mg Cholesterol; 11 g Carbohydrate; 1 g Fibre; 4 g Protein; 82 mg Sodium

tomato pineapple salad

Once the dressing's done—it can be stored in the fridge for up to five days—this salad can be made in minutes. For faster results, use kitchen scissors to cut up the basil.

Roma (plum) tomatoes, quartered lengthwise	6	6
Can of pineapple tidbits, drained	14 oz.	398 mL
Thinly sliced red onion	1/4 cup	60 mL
Chopped fresh basil (or 1 1/2 tsp., 7 mL, dried)	2 tbsp.	30 mL
CHILI GARLIC DRESSING		
Cooking oil	2 tbsp.	30 mL
White wine vinegar	2 tbsp.	30 mL
Garlic clove, minced (or 1/4 tsp., 1 mL, powder)	1	1
Dried crushed chilies	1/4 tsp.	1 mL
Salt	1/4 tsp.	1 mL
Pepper	1/4 tsp.	1 mL
Chopped pecans, toasted (see Tip, page 64)	1/3 cup	75 mL

Put first 4 ingredients into medium bowl. Toss gently.

Chili Garlic Dressing: Combine first 6 ingredients in jar with tight-fitting lid. Shake well. Makes about 1/4 cup (60 mL) dressing. Drizzle over tomato mixture. Toss gently.

Sprinkle pecans over top. Serves 6.

1 serving: 139 Calories; 9.8 g Total Fat (5.7 g Mono, 2.7 g Poly, 0.8 g Sat); 0 mg Cholesterol; 14 g Carbohydrate; 3 g Fibre; 2 g Protein; 112 mg Sodium

greek salad

For the traditional Greek experience you can use whole kalamata olives instead of the sliced black olives, and garnish with a few sardines or anchovies. All you need to make this a light meal is a basket of baguette slices.

Head of romaine lettuce, cut or torn	1	1
Head of iceberg lettuce, chopped or torn	1/2	1/2
English cucumber (with peel), cubed	1	1
Medium tomatoes, chopped	2	2
Cubed feta cheese (about 4 oz., 113 g)	3/4 cup	175 mL
Sliced black olives	1/4 cup	60 mL
Sliced green onion	1/4 cup	60 mL
GREEK DRESSING		
Cooking (or olive) oil	1/2 cup	125 mL
Chopped fresh parsley (or 1 tbsp., 15 mL, flakes)	1/4 cup	60 mL
Red wine vinegar	1/4 cup	60 mL
Dried oregano	1/8 tsp.	0.5 mL
Garlic powder	1/8 tsp.	0.5 mL
Salt	1/2 tsp.	2 mL
Pepper	1/8 tsp.	0.5 mL

Put romaine and iceberg lettuce into large bowl or arrange on large serving platter. Scatter next 5 ingredients over top.

Greek Dressing: Combine all 7 ingredients in jar with tight-fitting lid. Shake well. Makes about 3/4 cup (175 mL) dressing. Drizzle over lettuce mixture. Serves 6.

1 serving: 269 Calories; 24.3 g Total Fat (12.5 g Mono, 6.1 g Poly, 4.4 g Sat); 17 mg Cholesterol; 9 g Carbohydrate; 2 g Fibre; 6 g Protein; 468 mg Sodium

tomato mushroom salad

Because the dressing uses only dried herbs, you can keep it in the fridge for up to two weeks. Make double to have on hand when tomatoes are just falling off the vine.

Medium tomatoes, cut into 8 wedges each	3	3
Thickly sliced fresh white mushrooms	3 cups	750 mL
Medium red onion, thinly sliced	1	1
Slivered green pepper (optional)	1/2 cup	125 mL
HERB DRESSING		
Cooking oil	1/4 cup	60 mL
Red wine vinegar	1/4 cup	60 mL
Granulated sugar	1 1/2 tsp.	7 mL
Salt	1 tsp.	5 mL
Dried basil	1/2 tsp.	2 mL
Parsley flakes	1/2 tsp.	2 mL
Lemon pepper	1/4 tsp.	1 mL
Garlic powder	1/8 tsp.	0.5 mL

Put first 4 ingredients into large bowl. Toss.

Herb Dressing: Combine all 8 ingredients in jar with tight-fitting lid. Shake well. Makes about 1/2 cup (125 mL) dressing. Drizzle over tomato mixture. Toss. Let stand for at least 1 hour to blend flavours. Makes about 8 cups (2 L).

1 cup (250 mL): 110 Calories; 7.4 g Total Fat (4.0 g Mono, 2.1 g Poly, 0.5 g Sat); 0 mg Cholesterol; 10 g Carbohydrate; 1 g Fibre; 2 g Protein; 309 mg Sodium

creamy corn salad

Deliciously spiced and bursting with colour, this salad can be mixed a few hours before serving to let the flavours get to know each other.

Can of black beans, rinsed and drained	14 oz.	398 mL
Can of kernel corn, drained	12 oz.	341 mL
Medium tomatoes, seeds removed and finely chopped	2	2
Finely chopped red onion	1/2 cup	125 mL
Finely chopped red pepper	1/2 cup	125 mL
Chopped fresh cilantro or parsley (optional)	2 tbsp.	30 mL
SPICY RANCH DRESSING		
Ranch dressing	1/4 cup	60 mL
Lime juice	1 tbsp.	15 mL
Garlic clove, minced (or 1/4 tsp., 1 mL, powder)	1	1
Chili powder	1/4 tsp.	1 mL
Ground cumin	1/4 tsp.	1 mL
Salt	1/4 tsp.	1 mL

Put first 6 ingredients into large bowl. Toss.

Spicy Ranch Dressing: Combine all 6 ingredients in small bowl. Makes about 1/3 cup (75 mL) dressing. Drizzle over tomato mixture. Toss well. Serves 6.

1 serving: 150 Calories; 4.6 g Total Fat (2.3 g Mono, 1.6 g Poly, 0.4 g Sat); 3 mg Cholesterol; 24 g Carbohydrate; 4 g Fibre; 5 g Protein; 395 mg Sodium

veggie pasta salad

Grilled vegetables tossed with pasta in a creamy sun-dried tomato sauce. Fabulous!

Roma (plum) tomatoes, cut into 6 wedges	8	8
Chopped green onion	1/2 cup	125 mL
Balsamic vinegar	2 tbsp.	30 mL
Olive (or cooking) oil	2 tbsp.	30 mL
Garlic clove, minced (or 1/4 tsp., 1 mL, powder)	1	1
Granulated sugar	1/2 tsp.	2 mL
Italian no-salt seasoning	1/2 tsp.	2 mL
Salt, sprinkle		
Pepper, sprinkle		
Large red peppers, quartered	2	2
Medium zucchini (with peel), cut lengthwise into 1/4 inch (6 mm) thick slices	2	2
Eggplant (with peel), cut lengthwise into 1/4 inch (6 mm) thick slices	1	1
Cooked penne pasta (about 2 cups, 500 mL, uncooked), chilled	4 cups	1 L
Sour cream	1/3 cup	75 mL
Sun-dried tomato pesto	1/4 cup	60 mL

Put first 9 ingredients into medium bowl. Stir. Transfer to greased 8 x 8 inch (20 x 20 cm) foil pan. Preheat gas barbecue to medium-high. Place pan on ungreased grill. Close lid. Cook for about 15 minutes, stirring occasionally, until tomato is softened. Transfer tomato mixture with slotted spoon to large bowl. Discard liquid.

Cook red peppers on greased grill for about 15 minutes, turning occasionally, until grill marks appear and skins are slightly blackened. Transfer to cutting board. Chop coarsely. Add to tomato mixture.

Cook zucchini and eggplant slices on greased grill for 3 to 4 minutes per side until softened and grill marks appear. Transfer to cutting board. Chop coarsely. Add to tomato mixture. Add pasta. Toss gently.

Combine sour cream and pesto in small bowl. Add to pasta mixture. Toss gently. Makes about 10 cups (2.5 L). Serves 6.

1 serving: 292 Calories; 8.1 g Total Fat (4.1 g Mono, 1.1 g Poly, 2 g Sat); 5 mg Cholesterol; 50 g Carbohydrate; 7 g Fibre; 9 g Protein; 79 mg Sodium

summer gazpacho

This smooth, refreshing soup, balanced by the crunchy crouton garnish, makes a delightful start to a patio meal. Beer mugs, champagne flutes or even clear dessert bowls also make wonderful servers, as long as they're chilled before they're filled!

Baguette bread slices, 1 inch (2.5 cm) thick	2	2
Water, to cover		
Large tomatoes, peeled (see Tip, page 64), seeds removed and chopped	4	4
Chopped, peeled and seeded English cucumber	1 cup	250 mL
Chopped red pepper	1 cup	250 mL
Chopped red onion	1/2 cup	125 mL
Olive oil	2 1/2 tbsp.	37 mL
Red wine vinegar	2 1/2 tbsp.	37 mL
Lime juice	1 tbsp.	15 mL
Garlic clove, minced	1	1
Hot pepper sauce	1/2 tsp.	2 mL
Salt	1/2 tsp.	2 mL
Baguette bread slices, 1/2 inch (12 mm) thick	8	8
Olive oil	1 1/2 tsp.	7 mL

Put first amount of baguette slices into small bowl. Add water. Soak for about 5 minutes until very soft. Drain. Squeeze water from bread. Set aside.

Combine next 10 ingredients in large bowl. Process 3/4 cup (175 mL) tomato mixture in blender or food processor until finely chopped. Transfer to small bowl. Reserve and chill. Add wet bread to remaining tomato mixture. Process in blender or food processor until smooth. Chill, covered, for at least 2 hours until cold. Pour into 4 chilled bowls.

Arrange second amount of baguette slices on baking sheet. Brush with second amount of olive oil. Broil on top rack in oven for about 1 minute per side until golden. Place 2 slices on each bowl. Spoon reserved tomato mixture over bread. Serves 4.

1 serving: *337 Calories; 13.1 g Total Fat (8.5 g Mono, 1.7 g Poly, 1.9 g Sat); 0 mg Cholesterol; 50 g Carbohydrate; 6 g Fibre; 8 g Protein; 716 mg Sodium*

curry yogurt chicken
with tomato salsa

Inspired by South Asian flavours, this dish pairs well with rice or new potatoes.

Plain yogurt	1/2 cup	125 mL
Mild curry paste	1/4 cup	60 mL
Boneless, skinless chicken breast halves (4-6 oz., 113-170 g, each)	4	4

TOMATO SALSA		
Finely chopped tomato, seeds removed	2 cups	500 mL
Chopped red onion	1/2 cup	125 mL
Chopped fresh cilantro or parsley	1 tbsp.	15 mL
Olive oil	2 tsp.	10 mL
Lime juice	1/2 tbsp.	7 mL
Garlic clove, minced	1	1
Salt	1/4 tsp.	1 mL

Combine yogurt and curry paste in large bowl. Add chicken. Turn to coat. Preheat electric grill for 5 minutes or gas barbecue to medium. Cook on greased grill for 4 to 6 minutes per side until no longer pink.

Tomato Salsa: Combine all 7 ingredients in medium bowl. Makes about 3 cups (750 mL) salsa. Serve with chicken. Serves 4.

1 serving: 246 Calories; 9.2 g Total Fat (2.6 g Mono, 0.8 g Poly, 3.0 g Sat); 71 mg Cholesterol; 10 g Carbohydrate; 1 g Fibre; 28 g Protein; 766 mg Sodium

herbed spaghetti primavera

Use the season's freshest vegetables for this delicious, healthy dinner.
Parmesan cheese is an easy replacement for the Romano.

Olive (or cooking) oil	1 tbsp.	15 mL
Fresh peas	1 cup	250 mL
Small mushrooms	1 cup	250 mL
Garlic cloves, minced (or 1/2 tsp., 2 mL, powder)	2	2
Medium red pepper, slivered	1	1
Sliced zucchini (with peel)	1 cup	250 mL
Baby carrots, halved	8	8
Green onions, sliced	3	3
Dry (or alcohol-free) white wine	1/3 cup	75 mL
Half-and-half cream	2/3 cup	150 mL
Coarsely shredded fresh spinach leaves, lightly packed	1 cup	250 mL
Diced fresh tomato	1 cup	250 mL
Chopped fresh basil (or 3/4 tsp., 4 mL, dried)	1 tbsp.	15 mL
Chopped fresh dill (or 3/4 tsp., 4 mL, dried)	1 tbsp.	15 mL
Chopped fresh oregano (or 3/4 tsp., 4 mL, dried)	1 tbsp.	15 mL
Chopped fresh parsley (or 3/4 tsp., 4 mL, flakes)	1 tbsp.	15 mL
Salt	1/2 tsp.	2 mL
Pepper, sprinkle		

Grated Romano cheese	1/3 cup	75 mL
Water	12 cups	3 L
Salt	1 tbsp.	15 mL
Spaghetti	12 oz.	340 g
Grated Romano cheese	2 tbsp.	30 mL

Heat wok or large frying pan on medium-high until very hot. Add olive oil. Add next 3 ingredients. Stir-fry for 1 minute.

Add next 4 ingredients. Stir-fry for 2 to 3 minutes until vegetables are brightly coloured.

Add wine. Cook for 1 minute. Add cream. Cover. Bring to a boil. Reduce heat to medium-low. Cook for 3 to 4 minutes until vegetables are tender-crisp.

Add next 8 ingredients. Stir. Cover. Bring to a boil. Reduce heat to medium-low. Simmer for about 5 minutes until tomato is soft. Stir in first amount of cheese.

Combine water and salt in large saucepan or Dutch oven. Bring to a boil. Add spaghetti. Boil, uncovered, for 9 to 10 minutes, stirring occasionally, until tender but firm. Drain. Transfer to serving dish. Add vegetable mixture. Toss gently. Sprinkle with second amount of cheese. Serves 6.

1 serving: 367 Calories; 8.7 g Total Fat (3.3 g Mono, 1.0 g Poly, 3.7 g Sat); 17 mg Cholesterol; 57 g Carbohydrate; 5 g Fibre; 15 g Protein; 328 mg Sodium

smothered halibut

Boil up some rice or new potatoes while the fish is baking and dinner's done.

Halibut fillets, bones removed and cut into 4 equal pieces	1 1/4 lbs.	560 g
Butter (or hard margarine)	1 1/2 tsp.	7 mL
Large onion, thinly sliced and separated into rings	1	1
Butter (or hard margarine)	1 1/2 tsp.	7 mL
Medium carrot, grated	1	1
Medium parsnip, grated	1	1
Small zucchini (with peel), thinly sliced lengthwise	1	1
Medium tomatoes, seeds removed and diced	2	2
Dried basil	3/4 tsp.	4 mL
Salt	1/2 tsp.	2 mL
Pepper	1/4 tsp.	1 mL
Grated Parmesan cheese	2 tbsp.	30 mL

Arrange fish in greased 8 x 8 inch (20 x 20 cm) pan.

Melt first amount of butter in small frying pan on medium. Add onion. Cook for 5 to 10 minutes, stirring often, until softened. Scatter over fish.

Melt second amount of butter in same pan. Add carrot and parsnip. Cook for about 2 minutes, stirring often, until tender. Scatter over onion.

Cook zucchini in same pan for about 2 minutes, stirring often, until softened. Arrange on carrot mixture.

Put tomato into medium bowl. Sprinkle with next 3 ingredients. Toss until coated. Scatter over zucchini.

Sprinkle with cheese. Cover with greased foil. Bake in 450°F (230°C) oven for 30 to 35 minutes until fish flakes easily when tested with a fork. Serves 4.

1 serving: 266 Calories; 7.6 g Total Fat (2.3 g Mono, 1.5 g Poly, 3.0 g Sat); 55 mg Cholesterol; 17 g Carbohydrate; 4 g Fibre; 33 g Protein; 331 mg Sodium

chicken in wine sauce

If you're busy on the day guests are to arrive, make this casserole the day before.
Simply reheat in a 300°F (150°C) oven for 30 minutes or until heated through.

Olive (or cooking) oil	1 tbsp.	15 mL
Boneless, skinless chicken breast halves (4 – 6 oz., 113 – 170 g, each)	8	8
Olive (or cooking) oil	1 tbsp.	15 mL
Sliced fresh white mushrooms	1 cup	250 mL
Green onion, sliced	1	1
Garlic clove, minced (or 1/4 tsp., 1 mL, powder), optional	1	1
Dry (or alcohol-free) white wine	1 cup	250 mL
Chopped seeded tomato	1 cup	250 mL
Finely shredded basil (or 3/4 tsp., 4 mL, dried)	1 tbsp.	15 mL
Chopped fresh rosemary (or 1/4 tsp., 1 mL, dried, crushed)	1 tsp.	5 mL
Salt	1/2 tsp.	2 mL
Granulated sugar	1/4 tsp.	1 mL
Water	3 tbsp.	50 mL
Cornstarch	3 tbsp.	50 mL

Heat first amount of olive oil in large frying pan on medium. Add chicken. Cook for about 3 minutes per side until browned. Arrange in ungreased 2 quart (2 L) casserole.

Heat second amount of olive oil in same frying pan. Add next 3 ingredients. Cook for 3 to 5 minutes until green onion is softened. Stir in wine. Bring to a boil. Reduce heat to medium. Boil gently, uncovered, for 10 to 15 minutes until slightly reduced.

Add next 5 ingredients. Stir. Pour over chicken. Bake, covered, in 350°F (175°C) oven for about 45 minutes until chicken is no longer pink inside. Remove chicken to serving platter with slotted spoon. Cover to keep warm. Strain liquid into small saucepan, reserving solids. Bring to a boil.

Stir water into cornstarch in small cup. Add to saucepan. Heat and stir on medium until bubbling and thickened. Add reserved solids. Stir. Pour over chicken. Serves 8.

1 serving: 196 Calories; 5.5 g Total Fat (3 g Mono, 0.8 g Poly, 1 g Sat); 66 mg Cholesterol; 5 g Carbohydrate; trace Fibre; 26 g Protein; 152 mg Sodium

summer tomato and cheese sauce

Served over hot pasta, this sauce is divine, and wonderfully forgiving on the waistline! For a casual get-together, just add a starter, a salad and a store-bought dessert. Summertime...and the entertaining is easy!

Diced, seeded Roma (plum) tomato	3 cups	750 mL
Shredded fresh basil, lightly packed (or 1 tbsp., 15 mL, dried)	1/4 cup	60 mL
Thinly sliced green onion	1/4 cup	60 mL
Olive (or cooking) oil	1 tbsp.	15 mL
Garlic cloves, minced (or 1/2 tsp., 2 mL, powder)	2	2
Salt	1/2 tsp.	2 mL
Pepper, sprinkle		
Diced roasted red pepper (optional)	2/3 cup	150 mL
Low-fat cottage cheese, mashed with fork	1 cup	250 mL
Grated light Parmesan cheese	1 tbsp.	15 mL

Combine first 8 ingredients in medium saucepan. Let stand, covered, at room temperature for at least 1 hour to blend flavours. Simmer, uncovered, on medium until heated through.

Add cottage and Parmesan cheeses. Stir. Makes about 3 cups (750 mL).

3/4 cup (175 mL): 117 Calories; 4.1 g Total Fat (2.7 g Mono, 0.5 g Poly, 0.7 g Sat); 1 mg Cholesterol; 8 g Carbohydrate; 2 g Fibre; 13 g Protein; 489 mg Sodium

tomato crowns

The zigzag cut gives these tomatoes a regal appearance, and is easier to do than you might think! Just follow our step-by-step directions. You can assemble these tomatoes up to 24 hours ahead of time and refrigerate in an airtight container. Bake as directed.

Medium Roma (plum) tomatoes	3	3
Fine dry bread crumbs	1/4 cup	60 mL
Chopped fresh parsley	1 tbsp.	15 mL
(or 3/4 tsp., 4 mL, flakes)		
Olive (or cooking) oil	1 tbsp.	15 mL
Small garlic clove, minced	1	1
(or 1/8 tsp., 0.5 mL, powder)		
Seasoned salt	1/8 tsp.	0.5 mLw

Slice 1/8 inch (3 mm) from both ends of each tomato. Cut tomatoes in half in zigzag pattern by inserting small sharp knife though tomato skin to centre of flesh. Cut repeating W-shaped pattern around circumference (inset photo). Arrange in greased 1 quart (1 L) shallow baking dish.

Combine remaining 5 ingredients in small bowl. Spoon over crowns. Bake, uncovered, in 375°F (190°C) oven for about 15 minutes until crumb mixture is golden. Makes 6 crowns.

1 Crown: *53 Calories; 2.8 g Total Fat (1.8 g Mono, 0.4 g Poly, 0.4 g Sat); 0 mg Cholesterol; 7 g Carbohydrate; 1 g Fibre; 1 g Protein; 73 mg Sodium*

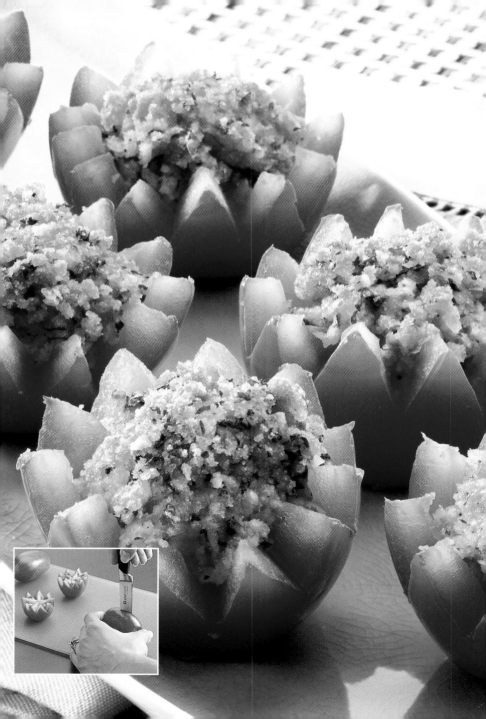

baked stuffed tomatoes

The sooner you get a firm, ripe tomato off the vine and into this dish, the more flavourful it will be. Sprigs of fresh herbs make an eye-catching garnish.

Medium tomatoes	6	6
Grated sharp Cheddar cheese	1/2 cup	125 mL
Fine dry bread crumbs	1/4 cup	60 mL
Tomato paste	1/4 cup	60 mL
Granulated sugar	1 tsp.	5 mL
Dried basil	1/4 tsp.	1 mL
Dried oregano	1/4 tsp.	1 mL
Salt	1/2 tsp.	2 mL
Pepper	1/16 tsp.	0.5 mL
Cooked long grain white rice (1/3 cup, 75 mL, uncooked)	1 cup	250 mL

Slice 1/4 inch (6 mm) from stem end of each tomato. Scoop out pulp. Set aside tomato shells. Coarsely chop pulp. Strain, discarding juice. Transfer pulp to medium bowl.

Add next 8 ingredients. Stir.

Add rice. Stir. Spoon into tomato shells. Place in greased 9 x 9 inch (22 x 22 cm) pan. Bake, uncovered, in 350°F (175°C) oven for 30 to 35 minutes until heated through and tomatoes are tender. Serves 6.

1 serving: 145 Calories; 4.2 g Total Fat (1.1 g Mono, 0.4 g Poly, 2.3g Sat); 10 mg Cholesterol; 22 g Carbohydrate; 2 g Fibre; 6 g Protein; 321 mg Sodium

tomato bean dish

While the red and green colours make this a great dish for festive occasions, tomato lovers and vegetarians will want to make it year round!

Frozen whole green beans, cooked and drained	6 cups	1.5 L
Medium tomatoes, chopped	6	6
Grated medium (or sharp) Cheddar cheese	2 cups	500 mL
Large eggs	4	4
Biscuit mix	1 cup	250 mL
Milk	1 cup	250 mL
Dried basil	1 tsp.	5 mL
Salt	1 tsp.	5 mL
Cayenne pepper	1/2 tsp.	2 mL

Arrange green beans in 9 x 13 inch (22 x 33 cm) pan. Scatter tomato over top. Sprinkle with cheese.

Beat eggs in large bowl until frothy. Add next 5 ingredients. Beat until smooth. Pour over cheese. Bake, uncovered, in 350°F (175°C) oven for about 50 minutes until knife inserted in centre comes out clean. Serves 10.

1 serving: 279 Calories; 14.3 g Total Fat (4.9 g Mono, 0.9 g Poly, 6.7 g Sat); 100 mg Cholesterol; 25 g Carbohydrate; 3 g Fibre; 13 g Protein; 678 mg Sodium

quick salsa

A food processor makes fast work of this salsa. To make a chunkier version, process the ingredients for only a few seconds. Ideal with tortilla chips or as a side for barbecued meats, this salsa can be refrigerated for up to a week.

Jalapeño pepper, halved (see Tip, page 64)	1	1
Small garlic clove	1	1
Medium green or yellow pepper, cut into chunks	1/2	1/2
Medium red onion, cut into chunks	1/2	1/2
Medium Roma (plum) tomatoes, quartered	6	6
Ground cumin	1/8 tsp.	0.5 mL
Salt	1/2 tsp.	2 mL
Pepper, sprinkle		
Fresh cilantro or parsley, to taste (optional)		
Can of diced green chilies, drained	4 oz.	113 g
Lime juice	2 tsp.	10 mL

Process first 4 ingredients in food processor with on/off motion 8 to 10 times until coarsely chopped. Scrape down side.

Add next 5 ingredients. Process with on/off motion several times until desired texture. Transfer to medium bowl. Stir in chilies and lime juice. Let stand, covered, at room temperature for 1 hour to blend flavours. Makes about 3 1/2 cups (875 mL).

2 tbsp. (30 mL): 5 Calories; 0.1 g Total Fat (trace Mono, trace Poly, trace Sat); 0 mg Cholesterol; 1 g Carbohydrate; trace Fibre; trace Protein; 71 mg Sodium

fresh tomato relish

Add a generous helping of this tasty condiment to fish, chicken, roast beef or pork. You can also try it on burgers, grilled sausages or baked potatoes.

Chopped seeded Roma (plum) tomato,	1 cup	250 mL
Finely chopped green pepper	1/4 cup	60 mL
Finely chopped red onion	1/4 cup	60 mL
Chopped fresh parsley (or cilantro), or 1 1/4 tsp. (6 mL), flakes	1 1/2 tbsp.	25 mL
Chopped fresh basil (or 3/4 tsp., 4 mL, dried)	1 tbsp.	15 mL
Chopped fresh chives (or 1/4 tsp., 1 mL, dried)	1 1/2 tsp.	7 mL
Red wine vinegar	1 1/2 tsp.	7 mL
Garlic clove, minced (or 1/4 tsp., 1 mL, powder)	1	1
Hot pepper sauce	1/4 tsp.	1 mL
Salt	1/4 tsp.	1 mL
Pepper, sprinkle		

Combine all 11 ingredients in medium bowl. Let stand, covered, at room temperature for 2 hours to blend flavours. Makes about 1 1/3 cups (325 mL).

2 tbsp. (30 mL): 6 Calories; 0.1 g Total Fat (trace Mono, trace Poly, trace Sat); 0 mg Cholesterol; 1 g Carbohydrate; trace Fibre; trace Protein; 58 mg Sodium

green tomato and pear chutney

When fall frosts nip at the tomato plants and you've had your fill of fried green tomatoes, here's an unusual chutney that will put the rest of your unripened harvest to good use.

Medium green tomatoes (about 2 lbs., 900 g), chopped	7	7
Medium peeled pears, chopped	3	3
Medium onions, chopped	2	2
Brown sugar, packed	2 cups	500 mL
Malt vinegar	2 cups	500 mL
Golden raisins	1 cup	250 mL
Brown mustard seed	1/3 cup	75 mL
Ground coriander	1 tbsp.	15 mL
Ground cumin	1 tbsp.	15 mL
Ground ginger	1 tbsp.	15 mL
Salt	2 tsp.	10 mL

Combine all 11 ingredients in a large heavy saucepan or Dutch oven. Heat and stir on medium for 3 to 5 minutes until brown sugar is dissolved. Bring to a boil. Reduce heat to medium. Boil gently, uncovered, for about 50 minutes, stirring occasionally, until very thick. Remove from heat. Fill 6 hot sterile 1 cup (250 mL) jars to within 1/2 inch (12 mm) of top. Wipe rims of jars. Place sterile metal lids on jars and screw on metal bands fingertip tight. Do not over-tighten. Process in boiling water bath for 5 minutes (see Note). Remove jars. Cool. Chill after opening. Makes about 6 cups (1.5 L).

2 tbsp. (30 mL): 65 Calories; 0.5 g Total Fat (0.3 g Mono, 0.1 g Poly, trace Sat); 0 mg Cholesterol; 16 g Carbohydrate; 1 g Fibre; 1 g Protein; 102 mg Sodium

Note: Processing time is for elevations 1001 to 3000 feet (306 to 915 m) above sea level. Make adjustment for elevation in your area if necessary.

tomato, date and caramelized onion jam

We think of this delicious spread as a savoury jam. While it makes a great accompaniment to beef, pork or chicken, it's also wonderful served with a selection of cheeses, pâté and bread as an appetizer or light lunch.

Cooking oil	1 tbsp.	15 mL
Medium onions, thinly sliced	4	4
Brown sugar, packed	1/4 cup	60 mL
Red wine vinegar	3 tbsp.	50 mL
Large tomatoes (about 3 lbs., 1.4 kg), peeled (see Tip, page 64) and chopped	6	6
Pitted dates, chopped	3 cups	750 mL
Granulated sugar	4 cups	1 L
Lemon juice	1/2 cup	125 mL

Heat cooking oil in large frying pan on low. Add onion. Cook for about 20 minutes, stirring occasionally, until softened. Add brown sugar and vinegar. Cook for about 5 minutes, stirring occasionally, until brown sugar is dissolved. Set aside.

Combine tomato and dates in large heavy saucepan or Dutch oven. Bring to a boil. Reduce heat to medium. Boil gently, uncovered, for about 20 minutes, stirring occasionally, until dates are soft and mixture is thickened.

Add granulated sugar, lemon juice and onion mixture. Heat and stir on low for 3 to 5 minutes until granulated sugar is dissolved. Bring to a boil. Reduce heat to medium. Boil gently, uncovered, for 15 to 20 minutes, stirring occasionally, until jam gels when tested on small cold plate (see Tip, page 64). Remove from heat. Fill 8 hot sterile 1 cup (250 mL) jars to within 1/2 inch (12 mm) of top. Wipe rims of jars. Place sterile metal lids on jars and screw on metal bands fingertip tight. Do not over-tighten. Process in boiling water bath for 5 minutes (see Note). Remove jars. Cool. Chill after opening. Makes about 8 cups (2 L).

2 tbsp. (30 mL): 83 Calories; 0.3 g Total Fat (0.1 g Mono, 0.1 g Poly, trace Sat); 0 mg Cholesterol; 21 g Carbohydrate; 1 g Fibre; trace Protein; 2 mg Sodium

Note: Processing time is for elevations 1001 to 3000 feet (306 to 915 m) above sea level. Make adjustment for elevation in your area if necessary.

pineapple and tomato jam

The fresh pineapple complements the natural sweetness of the tomatoes in this gingery jam. Outstanding with fresh biscuits, French toast, crispy croissants or English muffins.

Small oranges	3	3
Medium lemons	2	2
Chopped fresh pineapple	3 cups	750 mL
Medium tomatoes (about 1 3/4 lbs., 790 g), peeled (see Tip, page 64) and chopped	6	6
Finely grated gingerroot	2 1/2 tsp.	12 mL
Ground allspice	1/2 tsp.	2 mL
Granulated sugar	3 2/3 cups	900 mL

Squeeze juice from oranges and lemons to get about 1 1/4 cups (300 mL) in total. Reserve seeds. Transfer to 6 inch (15 cm) square of double-layered cheesecloth. Draw up corners and tie with butcher's string.

Combine next 4 ingredients, juice and cheesecloth bag in large saucepan or Dutch oven. Bring to a boil. Reduce heat to medium. Simmer, covered, for 20 to 25 minutes until tomato is pulpy.

Add sugar. Heat and stir on medium for 3 to 5 minutes until sugar is dissolved. Bring to a boil. Reduce heat to medium. Boil gently, uncovered, for about 50 minutes, stirring occasionally, until jam gels when tested on small cold plate (see Tip, page 64). Remove from heat. Remove and discard cheesecloth bag. Fill 4 hot sterile 1 cup (250 mL) jars to within 1/2 inch (12 mm) of top. Wipe rims of jars. Place sterile metal lids on jars and screw on metal bands fingertip tight. Do not over-tighten. Process in boiling water bath for 5 minutes (see Note). Remove jars. Cool. Chill after opening. Makes about 4 cups (1 L).

2 tbsp. (30 mL): 105 Calories; 0.2 g Total Fat (trace Mono, 0.1 g Poly, trace Sat); 0 mg Cholesterol; 27 g Carbohydrate; trace Fibre; trace Protein; 3 mg Sodium

Note: Processing time is for elevations 1001 to 3000 feet (306 to 915 m) above sea level. Make adjustment for elevation in your area if necessary.

tomato marmalade

Grateful recipients of jars of this surprisingly tart, citrus-flavoured marmalade will taste summer's bounty in every spoonful. Make extra as wonderful hostess gifts or stocking stuffers.

Apple cider vinegar	1/4 cup	60 mL
Chopped tomato	4 cups	1 L
Granulated sugar	2 cups	500 mL
Medium oranges, with peel, finely chopped	2	2
Ground cinnamon	1 tsp.	5 mL

Pour vinegar over tomato in large saucepan. Let stand at least 8 hours or overnight. Drain well.

Add next 3 ingredients. Cook, uncovered, on low for about 2 hours, stirring occasionally, until thickened. Remove from heat. Fill 3 hot sterile 1 cup (250 mL) jars to within 1/2 inch (12 mm) of top. Wipe rims of jars. Place sterile metal lids on jars and screw on metal bands fingertip tight. Do not over-tighten. Process in boiling water bath for 15 minutes (see Note). Remove jars. Cool. Chill after opening. Makes about 3 cups (750 mL).

1 tbsp. (15 mL): 38 Calories; 0.1 g Total Fat (trace Mono, trace Poly, trace Sat); 0 mg Cholesterol; 10 g Carbohydrate; trace Fibre; trace Protein; 1 mg Sodium

Note: Processing time is for elevations 1001 to 3000 feet (306 to 915 m) above sea level. Make adjustment for elevation in your area if necessary.

recipe index

topical tips

Chili pepper protection: Hot peppers contain capsaicin in the seeds and ribs. Removing the seeds and ribs will reduce the heat. Wear rubber gloves when handling hot peppers and avoid touching your eyes. Wash your hands well.

Jam and jelly gel test: To make sure your jams, jellies and marmalades have reached the gelling point, remove them from heat, place a spoonful on a chilled plate and place it in the freezer until the mixture has reached room temperature. Press the length of your finger down the middle of the mixture. If it doesn't run together into the "trench" you've created, the mixture has gelled. **Note:** Don't leave jams or jellies simmering on the stove while you're testing, to prevent overcooking.

Peeling tomatoes: Cut an 'X' through the skin on the bottom. Plunge them into boiling water for about 30 seconds, then remove them to a bowl of ice water. Peel skin away.

Storing garlic: Fresh garlic should be stored at room temperature in a cool, dry place. Refrigeration will dehydrate the cloves, affecting the garlic's flavour, and may result in other refrigerated foods absorbing its odour.

Storing tomatoes: To maintain optimum flavour, store tomatoes at room temperature. Refrigeration will stop the ripening process and alter flavour and texture.

Toasting nuts, seeds or coconut: Cooking times will vary for each type of nut, so never toast them together. For small amounts, place ingredient in an ungreased shallow frying pan. Heat on medium for three to five minutes, stirring often, until golden. For larger amounts, spread ingredient evenly in an ungreased shallow pan. Bake in a 350°F (175°C) oven for five to 10 minutes, stirring or shaking often, until golden.

Nutrition Information Guidelines

Each recipe is analyzed using the Canadian Nutrient File from Health Canada, which is based on the United States Department of Agriculture (USDA) Nutrient Database.

- If more than one ingredient is listed (such as "butter or hard margarine"), or if a range is given (1 – 2 tsp., 5 – 10 mL), only the first ingredient or first amount is analyzed.

- For meat, poultry and fish, the serving size per person is based on the recommended 4 oz. (113 g) uncooked weight (without bone), which is 2 – 3 oz. (57 – 85 g) cooked weight (without bone) — approximately the size of a deck of playing cards.

- Milk used is 1% M.F. (milk fat), unless otherwise stated.

- Cooking oil used is canola oil, unless otherwise stated.

- Ingredients indicating "sprinkle," "optional," or "for garnish" are not included in the nutrition information.

- The fat in recipes and combination foods can vary greatly depending on the sources and types of fats used in each specific ingredient. For these reasons, the count of saturated, monounsaturated and polyunsaturated fats may not add up to the total fat content.